PIANO • VOCAL • GUITAR

ROD STEWART
Storyteller

© 1994 WARNER BROS. PUBLICATIONS INC.
All Rights Reserved

Printed in Canada

ROD STEWART
Storyteller

CONTENTS

BABY JANE

Words and Music by ROD STEWART
and JAY DAVIS

Ba - **by Jane,** don't leave me hang - in' on the
Ba - **by Jane,** don't it make you feel
Ba - **by Jane,** I've said all I want to

line. I knew you when you had
sad. Just when I thought that
say Go your own way, don't

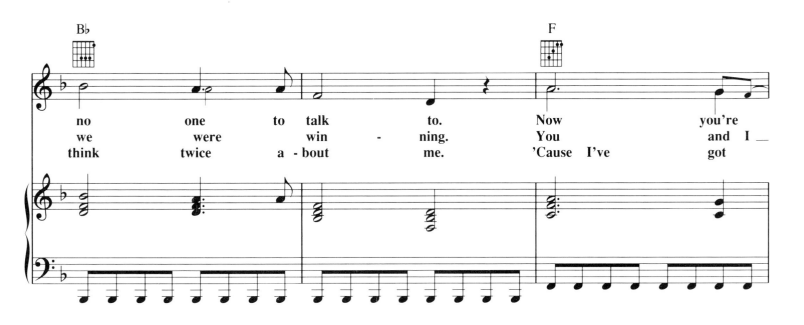

no one to talk to. Now you're
we were win - ning. You and I
think twice a - bout me. 'Cause I've got

mov - ing ___ in high so - ci - e - ty. ___
___ were so close in ev - 'ry way. ___
i - deas ___ and plans of my own. ___

Don't ___ for - get, I know se - crets a -
Don't ___ time ___ fly when your love ain't a a
So ___ long ___ dar - ling, I'll miss you, be -

ANGEL

Words and Music by
JIMI HENDRIX

An - gel came down from heav - en yes - ter - day___
Sure e - nough, this morning came un - to me___

stayed may - be long e-nough to res - cue me.
silver wings silhou-et-ted 'gainst a child's sun - rise

COUNTRY COMFORT

Words and Music by ELTON JOHN
and BERNIE TAUPIN

- forts and _ the road _ that's go - in' home, _ coun - try com-

- forts and _ the road _ that's go - in' home, _ coun - try com-

- forts and the road _ that's go - in' home, _ coun - try com -

no chord

- forts and the road _ that's go - in' home. _

CUT ACROSS SHORTY

Words and Music by MARIJOHN WILKIN
and WAYNE WALKER

prove who could run the fast - est   to win Miss Lu - cy's hand. __
made up his mind __ old Short - y   would end in sec - ond place. __

Now Dan __ had all __ the mon - ey   and he
You know Dan __ with his long legs fly - in'   he left
__ like that old sto - ry   a - bout the

al - so had the looks.   But Short - y must __ of had that
Short - y far __ be - hind.   But Short - y heard __ him
tur - tle and __ the hare,   when Dan __ crossed o - ver the

Now

But Short - y was - n't wor - ried. There was a

smile up - on his face 'cause old Lu - cy had fixed the race.

CRAZY ABOUT HER

Words and Music by ROD STEWART,
DUANE HITCHINGS and JIM CREGAN

I walk the streets at _ night un - til the morn - ing _ light comes
off my _ mind. I'm drink -ing too much _ wine. I'm burn-ing
ev - 'ry _ day in rush hour or sub - way, in a
longed to _ me I'd give her ev - 'ry - thing. I'd nev - er

no chord

Spoken: Every night I stand outside her door and wait for her to come by.

She lives in one of those brown-stones they guard outside and the limousines and the Rolls Royces comin' and goin'.

My friends all say she's way outta my class but I know if she'd just get to know me I could give her something all those

Gm   F7sus   Gm

rich guys ain't got.

Repeat and Fade

DA YA THINK I'M SEXY?

Words and Music by ROD STEWART,
CARMINE APPICE and DUANE HITCHINGS

DOWNTOWN TRAIN

Words and Music by
TOM WAITS

DRINKING AGAIN
(AKA "I'VE BEEN DRINKING")

Words by JOHNNY MERCER
Music by DORIS TAUBER

EVERY PICTURE TELLS A STORY

Words and Music by ROD STEWART
and RON WOOD

2. Paris was a place you could hide away, if you felt you didn't fit in.
French police wouldn't give me no peace, they claimed I was a nasty person.
Down along the Left Bank, minding my own, was knocked down by a human stampede;
Got arrested for inciting a peaceful riot, when all I wanted was a cup of tea.
I was accused.

3. I moved on.
Down in Rome I wasn't getting enough of the things that keep a young man alive.
My body stunk, but I kept my funk at a time when I was right out of luck.
Getting desperate, indeed I was looking like a tourist attraction.
Oh, my dear, I better get out of here for the Vatican don't give no sanction.
I wasn't ready for that, no, no.

4. I moved right out East, yeah!
On the Peking ferry I was feeling merry, sailing on my way back here.
I fell in love with a slant-eyed lady by the light of an eastern moon.
Shanghai Lil never used the pill, she claimed that it just ain't natural.
She took me up on deck and bit my neck. Oh, people, I was glad I found her,
Oh, yeah, I was glad I found her.

5. I firmly believed that I didn't need anyone but me.
I sincerely thought I was so complete. Look how wrong you can be.
The women I've known I wouldn't let tie my shoe. They wouldn't give you the time of day,
But the slant-eyed lady knocked me off my feet. God, I was glad I found her.

6. And if they had the words I could tell to you to help you on your way down the road,
I couldn't quote you no Dickens, Shelley or Keats, 'cause it's all been said before.
Make the best out of the bad, just laugh it off.
You didn't have to come here anyway. So remember: [To final ending]

EVERY BEAT OF MY HEART

Words and Music by ROD STEWART
and KEVIN SAVIGAR

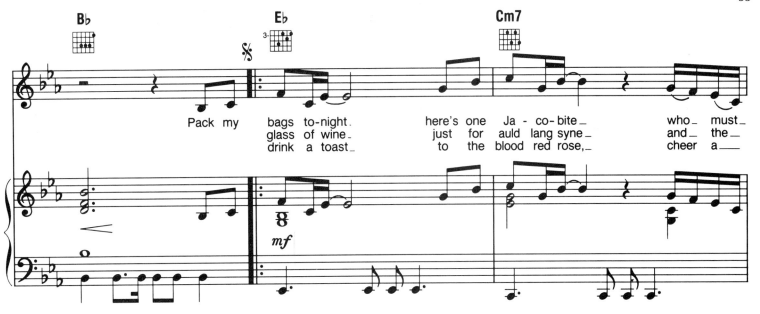

Pack my bags to-night.
glass of wine
drink a toast

here's one Ja - co - bite
just for auld lang syne
to the blood red rose,

who must
and the
cheer a

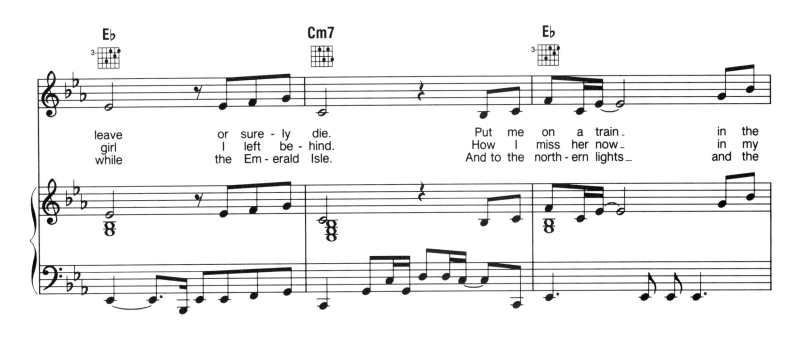

leave
girl
while

or sure - ly die.
I left be - hind.
the Em - erald Isle.

Put me on a train.
How I miss her now
And to the north - ern lights

in the
in my
and the

pour - ing rain
dark - est hour,
swirl - ing pipes,

say fare - well
and the way
how they make

but don't say good - bye.
our arms en - twine.
a grown man cry.

THE FIRST CUT IS THE DEEPEST

Slowly, with a beat

Words and Music by
CAT STEVENS

I would have
giv-en you all of my heart, but there's some-one who's torn it a-part.
want you by my side just to help me dry the tears that I've cried.

And she's tak-en just all that I had, but if you want, I'll
And I'm sure gon-na give you a try, and if you want, I'll

try to love a-gain. Ba-by, I'll try to love a-gain but I know:
try to love a-gain. Ba-by, I'll try to love a-gain but I know:

FOREVER YOUNG

Words and Music by ROD STEWART, JIM CREGAN
KEVIN SAVIGAR and BOB DYLAN

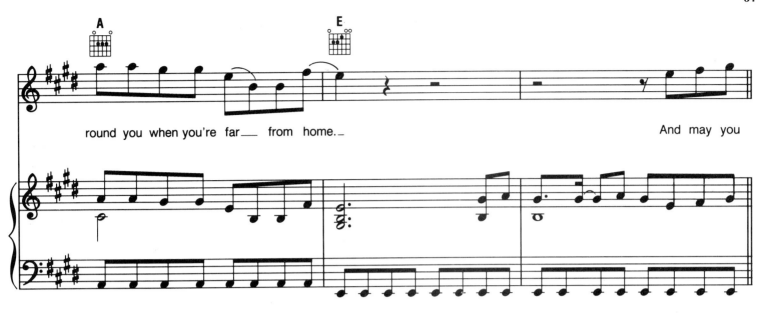

round you when you're far___ from home.___

And may you

grow___ to be proud,___ dig - ni - fied___ and true.___
for - tune be with you, may your guid - ing light___ be strong,___
fi - n'lly fly a - way, I'll be hoping that I served___ you well.___

And do un - to oth - ers as
build a stair - way to hea - ven with a
For all the wis - dom of a life - time,

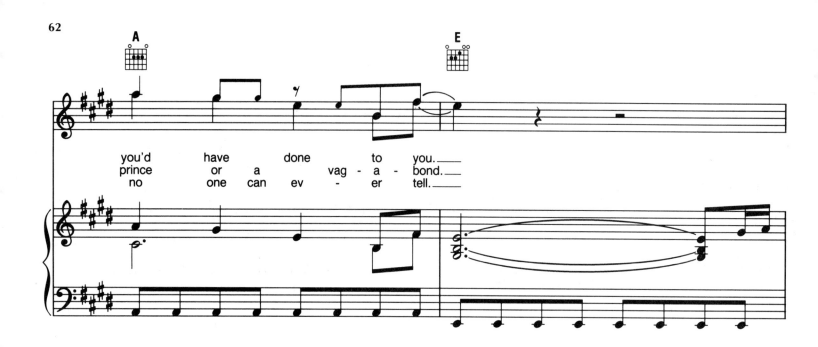

you'd have done to you.____
prince or a vag - a - bond.____
no one can ev - er tell.____

And

Be cou - ra - geous and____ be brave.____
And may you nev - er love____ in vain.____
But what - ev - er road____ you choose,____

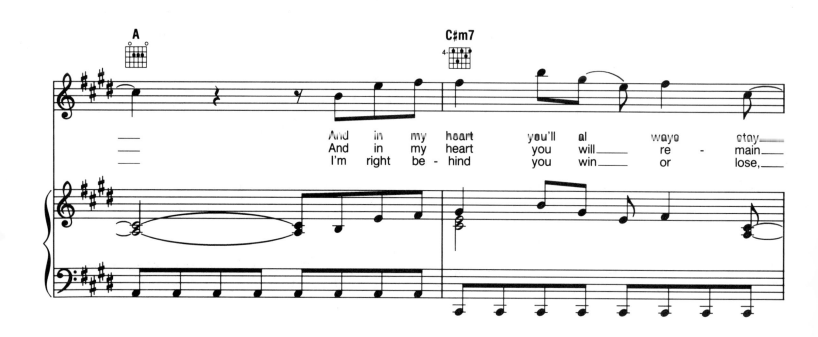

____ And in my heart you'll al - ways stay____
____ And in my heart you will____ re - main____
____ I'm right be - hind you win____ or lose,____

GASOLINE ALLEY

Words and Music by ROD STEWART
and RON WOOD

born to lead, bet - ter swal - low all my sil - ly coun - try pride.
catch you in the train. I'll be home be - fore the milk's up - on the door.

Go -

- in' home, _ run - nin' home, _ down the Gas - o - line Al - ley where I

start - ed from. _ Go - in' home, _ and I'm run - nin' home, _ down the

Gas-o-line Al - ley where I _____ was born. _

But if

GET BACK

Words and Music by JOHN LENNON
and PAUL McCARTNEY

GOOD MORNING LITTLE SCHOOLGIRL

By SONNY BOY WILLIAMSON

Can I ____ come home _____ with you? ____
what in the world_____ to do. ____
Fly____ right o - ver the town. ____

Tell ___ your
Well ___ I
If ___ I

moth - er and ___ your pa - pa   I once was a
don't want to hurt your feel - ings,   or e - ven get
don't find ___ my ba - by   ain't gon - na

I'm gon- na buy me an

D.S. al Coda

CODA

HANDBAGS AND GLADRAGS

By MICHAEL D'ABO

Medium Ballad Tempo

1. Ev - er seen a blind man cross the road tryin' to make the oth - er side?
2. Once I was a young man, and all I thought I had to do was smile.

you.

Hmm.

rit.

HOT LEGS

**Words and Music by
ROD STEWART**

You got legs right up to your neck.___ You're mak-in'

me a phys-i-cal wreck.___ I'm talk-in' to you:

Hot legs, in your sat-in shoes.___ Hot legs, are you

Hot legs, you're mak-in' your mark.___ Hot legs, keep my

Hot legs, you're wear-in' me out.___ Hot legs, you can

still in   school?_   Hot legs, you're mak-in' me a   fool._
pen-cil   sharp._   Hot legs,   keep your   hands to your-self._
scream and shout._   Hot legs,   you're still in   school._

1. 2.
Tacet   N.C.

I   love you, hon-ey.
I   love you, hon-ey.

3.
Tacet   N.C.

I   love you, hon-ey.

G
xooo

Hot   legs.

Hot   legs.

Hot   legs.

Tacet

I love you, hon - ey._____

I AIN'T SUPERSTITIOUS

Words and Music by
WILLIE DIXON

I DON'T WANT TO TALK ABOUT IT

Words and Music by DANNY WHITTEN

(I KNOW) I'M LOSING YOU

By CORNELIUS GRANT
NORMAN WHITFIELD and EDDIE HOLLAND

I WAS ONLY JOKING

Words and Music by ROD STEWART
and GARY GRAINGER

I'D RATHER GO BLIND

By ELLINGTON JORDAN
and BILLY FOSTER

INFATUATION

Words and Music by ROD STEWART,
DUANE HITCHINGS and ROWLAND ROBINSON

Solid rock tempo

Ear-ly in the mor-nin' I __ can't __ sleep.
Caught me down __ like a kil - ler shark. __
Heart beats sil - ly like a big bass drum.

It's like a

THE KILLING OF GEORGIE
(PART I AND II)

Words and Music by
ROD STEWART

2. His mother's tears fell in vain
   The afternoon George tried to explain
   That he needed love like all the rest.
   Pa said, "There must be a mistake.
   How can my son not be straight
   After all I've said and done for him?"

3. Leavin' home on a Greyhound bus,
   Cast out by the ones he loves,
   A victim of these gay days it seems.
   Georgie went to New York town
   Where he quickly settled down
   And soon became the toast of the Great White Way.

4. Accepted by Manhattan's elite
   In all the places that were chic,
   No party was complete without George.
   Along the boulevards he'd cruise
   And all the old queens blew a fuse;
   Everybody loved Georgie boy.

5. The last time I saw George alive
   Was in the summer of '75.
   He said he was in love; I said, "I'm pleased."
   George attended the opening night
   Of another Broadway hype,
   But split before the final curtain fell.

6. Deciding to take a shortcut home,
   Arm in arm, they meant no wrong;
   A gentle breeze blew down Fifth Avenue.
   Out of a darkened side street came
   A New Jersey gang with just one aim:
   To roll some innocent passerby.

7. There ensued a fearful fight;
   Screams rung out in the night.
   Georgie's head hit a sidewalk cornerstone.
   A leather kid, a switchblade knife,
   He did not intend to take his life;
   He just pushed his luck a little too far that night.

8. The sight of blood dispersed the gang;
   A crowd gathered, the police came,
   An ambulance screamed to a halt on Fifty-third and Third.
   Georgie's life ended there,
   But I ask, who really cares?
   George once said to me, and I quote:

9. He said: "Never wait or hesitate.
   Get in, kid, before it's too late;
   You may never get another chance,
   Cause youth's a mask, but it don't last.
   Live it long and live it fast."
   Georgie was a friend of mine.

LITTLE MISS UNDERSTOOD

By MICHAEL D' ABO

stood, _____ that's all

D.S. al Coda

CODA

that's all.

Hoo _____

LET ME BE YOUR CAR

Words and Music by ELTON JOHN
and BERNIE TAUPIN

LOVE TOUCH
(Theme from LEGAL EAGLES)

Words and Music by MIKE CHAPMAN,
HOLLY KNIGHT and GENE BLACK

love's worth one more try. __ Don't push it all a - side, __ 'cause I want to be

good for you. __ I did-n't mean to be bad. But dar - lin' I'm still the best __ that you

ev - er had. __ Just give me a chance __ to let me show you how

much. I want to give you my love __ touch. __

Eb **Ab** **Eb** **Ab** **Eb** **Ab** **Eb**

To Coda

I want to give you my love_ touch._

Why can't I climb_ your walls and find_ some-where to hide?_
This ev-er chang-ing love is push-ing me too far;

Can't I_ knock down_ your door and drag_ my-self in-side? _____
I feel a need to reach you right now where-ev-er you are. _____

I'll light your can-dles, and ba-by, may-be I'll light_ your life._
These emp-ty arms are get-ting strong-er ev-ery day._

LOST IN YOU

Words and Music by ROD STEWART
and ANDY TAYLOR

CODA

you.)   Hey!

A♭   E♭

A♭

(Spoken first time:)   I miss you, baby. (I miss you, too.)

E♭

I miss your laugh-in' eyes. ___   I miss our   ba-by cryin'.

MAGGIE MAY

Words and Music by ROD STEWART
and MARTIN QUITTENTON

Medium Rock beat

1. Wake up, Mag-gie, I think I got some-thing to say to you.___ It's

late Sep-tem-ber and I real-ly should___ be back___ at___ school.___

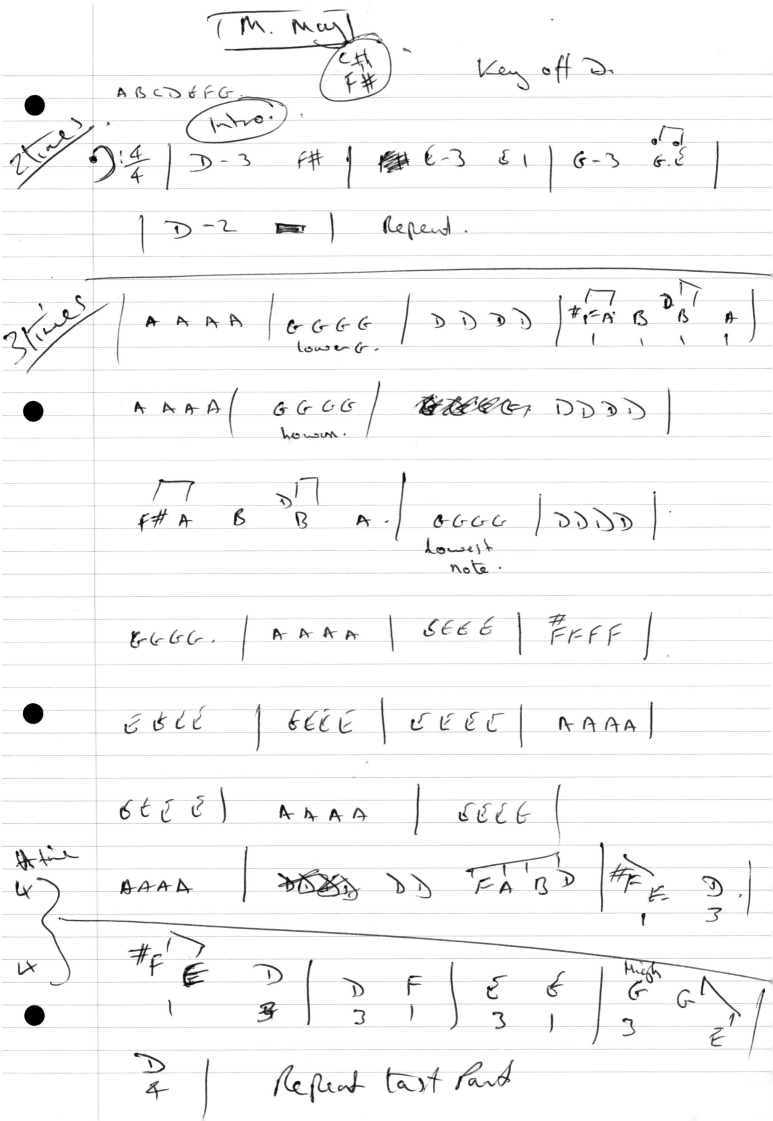

2. The morning sun, when it's in your face,
   Really shows your age.
   But that don't worry me none.
   In my eyes, you're everything.
   I laughed at all of your jokes.
   My love you didn't need to coax.
   Oh, Maggie, I couldn't have tried any more.
   You led me away from home
   Just to save you from being alone.
   You stole my soul, and that's a pain I can do without.

3. All I needed was a friend
   To lend a guiding hand.
   But you turned into a lover, and, mother, what a lover!
   You wore me out.
   All you did was wreck my bed,
   And, in the morning, kick me in the head.
   Oh, Maggie, I couldn't have tried any more.
   You led me away from home
   'Cause you didn't want to be alone.
   You stole my heart. I couldn't leave you if I tried.

4. I suppose I could collect my books
   And get on back to school.
   Or steal my daddy's cue
   And make a living out of playing pool.
   Or find myself a rock 'n' roll band
   That needs a helping hand.
   Oh, Maggie, I wish I'd never seen your face.
   You made a first-class fool out of me.
   But I'm as blind as a fool can be.
   You stole my heart, but I love you anyway.

MANDOLIN WIND

Words and Music by
ROD STEWART

2. Oh, the snow fell without a break,
   Buffalo died in the frozen fields, you know.
   Through the coldest winter in almost fourteen years
   I couldn't believe you kept a smile.
   Now I can rest assured, knowing that we've seen the worst,
   And I know I love ya.

3. Oh, I never was good with romantic words,
   So the next few lines come really hard.
   Don't have much, but what I've got is yours,
   Except, of course, my steel guitar.
   Ha, 'cause I know you don't play
   But I'll teach you one day
   Because I love ya.

4. I recall the night we knelt and prayed,
   Noticing your face was thin and pale.
   I found it hard to hide my tears,
   I felt ashamed, I felt I'd let ya down.
   No mandolin wind couldn't change a thing,
   Couldn't change a thing, no, no.

MY HEART CAN'T TELL YOU NO

Words and Music by SIMON CLIMIE
and DENNIS MORGAN

OH GOD, I WISH I WAS HOME TONIGHT

Words and Music by ROD STEWART, PHIL CHEN,
KEVIN SAVIGAR, JIM CREGAN and GARY GRAINGER

1. The rain poured down the wind swept a ven-ue

On a-noth-er dark wet Dec-ember af-ter-noon

VERSE 2: I would have wrote you a letter but telephone calls are free
'Cos the boys in the next apartment are working all day
They're a great bunch of guys but I think they're all gay
What am I doing avoiding what I'm trying to say.

Oh__ God__ I wish I was home__ to-night__ with you in my__ arms But

Oh__ God__ I wish I was home__ to-night__

VERSE 3: Send me a naked picture by the U.S. mail,
Write a pornographic letter you know I won't tell,
Keep your legs closed tight keep your body under lock and key,
Stay home at night and save all the best parts for me.
Yeah baby.

CHORUS 2: Oh God I wish I was home tonight, yes I do baby
Oh God I wish I was home tonight, oh

VERSE: *(Instrumental)*

VERSE 4: I could be home in time for christmas if you want me to be
There's a plane leaves here at midnight arriving at three
But I'm a bit financially embarrased I must admit
To tell you the truth my honey I haven't a cent.

CHORUS: Oh God I wish I was home tonight, tonight baby
Oh God I wish I was home tonight.

VERSE 5: Guess I'd better ring off before the boys get home,
My regards to all your family and everyone at home
There's a lump comes in my throat and a tear I can't hide
'Cos I want to see you so badly I just may die

CHORUS: Oh God I wish I was home tonight (with the ones that I love)
Oh God I wish I was home tonight.
Oh God I wish I was home tonight.
Oh my God I wish I was home tonight.

VERSE 6: I've been hearing voices out on the street,
They say you've found someone else who's really quite neat,
Bet he doesn't move you like I do
Tell me what I wanna hear that it just ain't true. *(fading)*

OH NO, NOT MY BABY

Words and Music by GERRY GOFFIN
and CAROLE KING

When my friends told___ me you had
My ma - ma told___ me, "Son when

some - one new, ___
ru - mors spread that there is

I did -n't be - lieve a sin - gle
truth some-where, and you should

word was true.___
use your head." _____

I told them all __ I had
But I sure did -n't lis - ten to

PASSION

Words and Music by ROD STEWART, PHIL CHEN
KEVIN SAVIGAR, JIM CREGAN and GARY GRAINGER

1. Some - bo - dy some-where___ in the heat of the night

look - ing pret-ty dan-ger-ous___ run-ning out of pa - tience.___

(2) To -

VERSE 2: Tonight in the city
You won't find any pity
Hearts are being twisted
Another lover cheated, cheated.

Instrumental: 8 bars of Em7

VERSE 4: New York, Moscow, passion, Hong Kong, Tokyo, passion
Paris and Bangkok, passion, a lotta people ain't got, passion.

VERSE 5: Hear it on the radio, passion, read it in the paper, passion,
Hear it in the churches, passion, see it in the school yards,
Passion.

MIDDLE: (Repeat) – 2 times

VERSE 6:   Alone in your bed at night, passion, it's half past midnight, passion
As you turn out your sidelight, passion, something ain't right, passion.

ENDING

There's no__ pas - sion   there's no__ pas - sion   there's__ no__

ENDING (*Cont.*) Passion, I need passion, you need passion.
We need passion, can't live without
Passion, won't live without passion,
Even the president needs passion,
Everybody I know needs some passion,
Some people die and kill for passion,
Nobody admits they need passion,
Some people are scared of passion,
Yeah passion.

PEOPLE GET READY

Words and Music by
CURTIS MAYFIELD

Moderately

Peo - ple get read - y, there's a train a - com - ing. You
Peo - ple get read - y, there's a train to Jor - dan.

don't need no bag - gage, you just get on board.__ All you need is faith __ to hear the
Pick - ing up pas - sen - gers from coast to coast.__ Faith is key, __ o - pen the

REASON TO BELIEVE

Words and Music by
TIM HARDIN

SAILING

Words and Music by
GAVIN SUTHERLAND

SHAPES OF THINGS

By PAUL SAMWELL-SMITH,
JAMES McCARTY and KEITH RELF

than   to -   day. _____

SO MUCH TO SAY

By MICHAEL D' ABO
and ROD STEWART

SOME GUYS HAVE ALL THE LUCK

Words and Music by
JEFF FORTGANG

With a steady beat

D.S. al Coda

Solo ends

CODA

But if you were here with me, ____

I'd feel so hap-py, I could cry.

You are so dear to me, __ I just can't __

Repeat and Fade

STAY WITH ME

Words and Music by RON WOOD
and ROD STEWART

STONE COLD SOBER

Words and Music by ROD STEWART
and STEVE CROPPER

197

SWEET LADY MARY

Words and Music by ROD STEWART,
RON WOOD and RON LANE

Steal a - way. ___

THIS OLD HEART OF MINE

By BRIAN HOLLAND, LAMONT DOZIER,
EDDIE HOLLAND and SYLVIA MOY

TO LOVE SOMEBODY

Words and Music by BARRY GIBB
and ROBIN GIBB

TONIGHT I'M YOURS
(DON'T HURT ME)

Words by
ROD STEWART
Music by KEVIN SAVIGAR
and JIM CREGAN

Medium beat

TONIGHT'S THE NIGHT
(Gonna Be Alright)

Words and Music by
ROD STEWART

WHAT AM I GONNA DO
(I'm So In Love With You)

Words and Music by ROD STEWART,
TONY BROCK and JAY DAVIS

TRUE BLUE

Words and Music by ROD STEWART
and RON WOOD

227

YOU CAN MAKE ME DANCE, SING OR ANYTHING

Words and Music by ROD STEWART, RON WOOD,
IAN McLAGEN, KENNY JONES and TETSU YAMAUCHI

YOU WEAR IT WELL

Words and Music by ROD STEWART
and MARTIN QUITTENTON

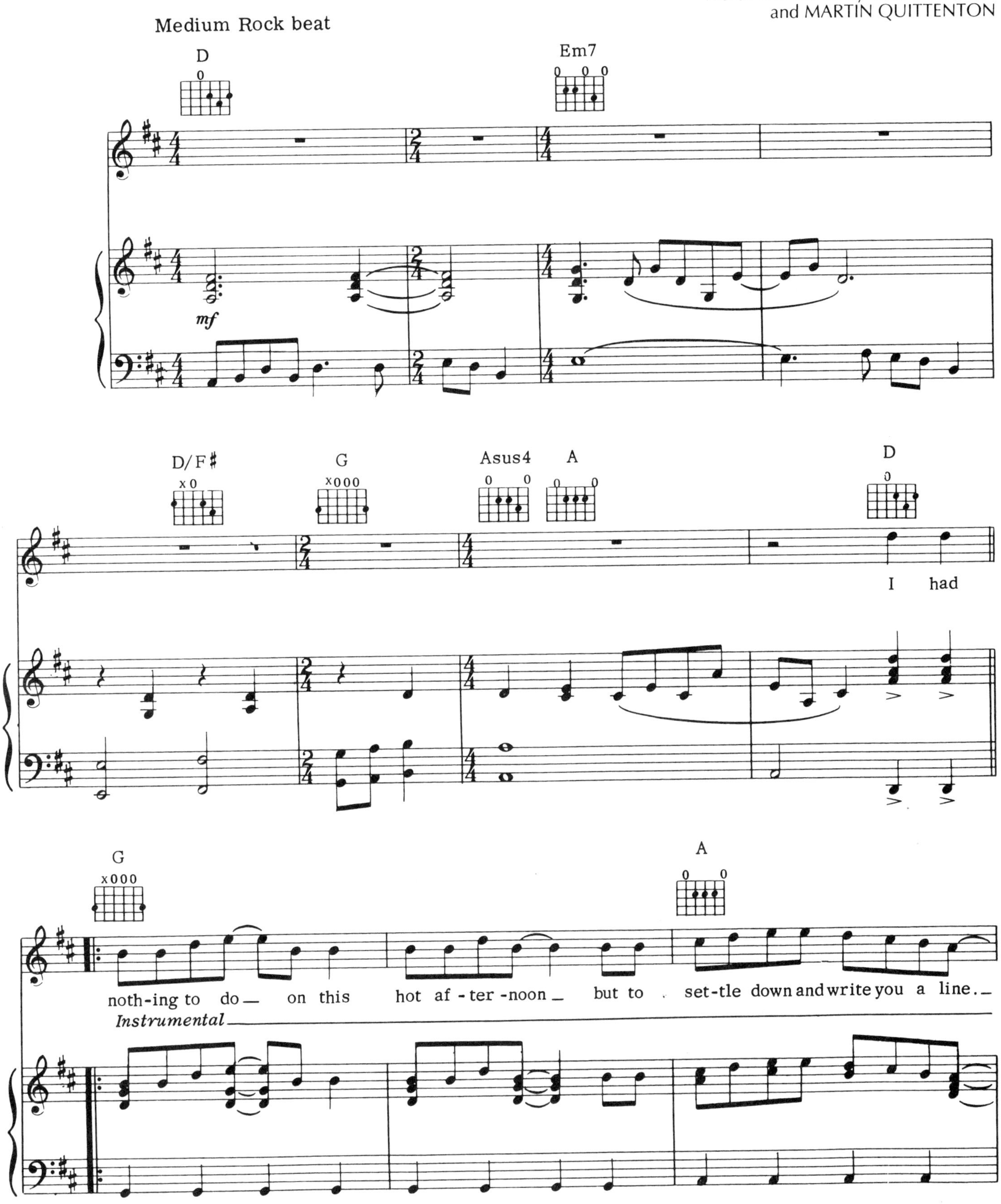

Medium Rock beat
D
Em7
mf
D/F♯
G
Asus4
A
D
I had
G
A
noth-ing to do — on this hot af-ter-noon — but to set-tle down and write you a line. —
Instrumental

YOU'RE IN MY HEART

Words and Music by
ROD STEWART

YOUNG TURKS

Words by ROD STEWART
Music by CARMINE APPICE,
KEVIN SAVIGAR adn DUANE HITCHINGS